A DISTANT HUM

ROBIN THOMAS

Cinnamon Press
:: small miracles from distinctive voices ::

Published by Cinnamon Press
www.cinnamonpress.com
Office 49019, PO Box 92, Cardiff, CF11 1NB

The right of Robin Thomas to be identified as author of this work has been asserted by him in accordance with the Copyright, Designs and Patent Act, 1988. Copyright © 2021 Robin Thomas.
ISBN: 978-1-78864-107-4

Designed and typeset in Palatino by Cinnamon Press.

Cover design by Adam Craig.

Cinnamon Press is represented in the UK by Inpress Ltd and in Wales by the Books Council of Wales.

Acknowledgments

Thanks to my many friends on the Reading and Bath poetry scenes and to Todd Swift, Jan Fortune and Adam Craig for their support, advice and encouragement.

Some of the poems appeared in my pamphlet *A Fury of Yellow* published by Eyewear in 2016

Thanks are also due to the editors of the following, in which some of these poems previously appeared: *Agenda, Envoi, Orbis, Brittle Star, Pennine Platform, The High Window, Poetry Scotland, South, Poetry Salzburg Review, Stand, Rialto, The Interpreters House, North* and the University of Reading Creative Arts Anthology

Thanks also to Ian House for his translation from Horace in 'A Tremendous Jape'.

Contents

The Lace Maker	9
The Project Manager	10
No. 29 Bus	11
Muskat Ramble	12
Tomorrows	13
University of Life	14
He Wishes to Make Use of the Big Bang	16
The Meaning of Barbie	17
Glass of Blessings	18
Paper Train	19
Afterlife	20
Head of Leon Kossof	21
A Man Embracing a Woman	22
Joao Gilberto in Rio	23
Billy Strayhorn's Journey	24
Pickpocket Poet	25
A Tremendous Jape	26
Petticoat	27
Let's Go!	28
Back the Attack	29
Divine Wind	30
One Fine Day	31
Interior with a Lady Choosing Fish	32
Brighton Pierrots	33
Cafferty's Lunch	34
Trains	35
Terra Nullius	36
Fawley Bottom	37
The Listening Girl	38
Over There	39
Bus	40
The Girl	41
Borders	42

Immaculate Conception 43

Conclusions 44

Intimations 45

The Bore 46

Excitement in the Garden 47

Abbey Quarter 48

Body and Soul 49

How to Write a Poem 50

Portrait 51

There is a Clifftop 52

Il Postino 53

The Heart's Reason 54

Dogs, Dead Game and Fruit 55

For Mary and Caitlin

A Distant Hum

The Lace Maker

Caspar Netscher, 1662

It's just a girl
wearing a black woollen skirt,
a red chemise
and a patterned cap.
She sits erect, her head
inclined to her work.
There's a besom, a picture, her shoes
and two oyster shells.

The painter loves her, well,
loves the colours of her clothes,
her shape against the luminous wall,
that there is nothing else,
except a seascape, a besom, two shoes
and are those oyster shells?
He can feel the weight of her on the chair.
All is calm and as it should be.

All is calm: her posture, the resting besom,
the grey wall, the unvarnished floorboards—
except that the storm,
detached from the wall in its violence,
has tossed her shoes aside
and thrown up oysters
which lie at her feet
like tiny unnoticed dogs.

The Project Manager

I have

created execution plans and mission statements whose aim was to deliver projects in accordance with customers' requirements and the company's long term objectives and have managed my projects in such a way as to fulfil my obligations in this respect,

presented reports to Management on the progress and financial status of my projects and confidently answered questions on these and other critical issues,

walked round construction sites looking important and knowledgeable,

had long discussions on the phone with people I had no wish to talk to,

been bad tempered under pressure,

eaten too much,

lied,

in the middle of the night, the rain drumming on the window, stayed awake with a problem, solved it, slipped back into restful sleep, only to forget the solution,

had a lizard fall into my beer,

been found out,

apologised.

No. 29 Bus

Eric Ravilious, 1934

On brick wheels,
routeless, unseamed,
untwentynined. Absent:
emerald green, cerulean blue,
vermillion, carmine, smalt.

Elsewhere,
upright, whole, proud,
No. 29 sallies forth
in Technicolor.

Muskat Ramble

i.m. Dobells Jazz Record Shop 1946-1980

He listens, pauses, provides an answer
from a store of knowledge unknown to me,
but beckoning. He leans over, taps
the stylus up, peers, sets it down just
there. Our air sparkles with electric sound.

All in this small, busy space are adult
except for us: two neat grammar school boys
fresh in from a decade not yet theirs.
In the basement, on top of the world,
I take the first steps into my own,
purchasing a second hand EP.

I played and played it,
wore grooves to neurons:
blues and rhythm and black and South
and a lustrous, piercing clarity.

Tomorrows

He is fishing in the shallows
of the swollen river. He turns
towards the bank, slips.
Amazement. Terror. 'Save me'
gargoyled in his face. Grabs.
Scrambles. Sits. Gasps.
Sandwiches, tea from a flask,
thoughts of the weather, tomorrow.

He is fishing in the shallows
of the swollen river. He turns
towards the bank, slips.
Amazement. Terror. 'Save me'
gargoyled in his face. Grabs.
Snap. Next day he's found,
wedged between boulders,
hair streaming, eyes vacant.

University of Life

I. New Worlds

Loaded with her life
we spin through normality,
land with a shudder,
open the doors to an alien place,
its angles, shadows, shapes
its very colours strange to us.
Our daughter,
her face set,
steps out,
signals 'Do not follow'.

I jab the return coordinates
Go in, go in!
    you bloody thing
        just when I need...
oh, right, and home, familiar, strange.
Our journey's now westward,
to clear and settle new frontiers.

II. Windows

We meet her among shop fronts
and corridors, concrete and neon.
We don't know what to do till lunch,
and afterwards, still don't know,
revisiting corridors, gazing
at things to buy until it's coffee time.
'I'll never make friends'. 'Never? You're
halfway through one term!' We look out
over the city. She's drinking tea, I note.

III. Birthday Treat

The tiered seats arrow to the
swirl of bodies, billowing colours.
Sound rises like poured perfume.
I'm sinking,

> *don't be cross, don't drive off*
> *he's not out yet! stupid, my*
> *face burning, why would I say*
> *that, no Schnurman's ok, but*
> *I have to go,*

> *Bye bye, night night.*
> *Are you on the pomputer?*
> *Don't go yet, Daddy.*
> *Wish I'd spent more time*
> *now she's gone.*

End of act I, the swans' wings fold.
'Did you enjoy it, Dad? Isn't it the best ever?'

He wishes to make use of the Big Bang

Were the expanding universe—
enwrought with bosons, leptons, quarks
across its great expanse—in my purview,
I would leap its whirling immensity,
yea its planets, galaxies and stars,
my head spinning, my heart aflame,
you intergalactically to avoid.

The Meaning of Barbie

A 'B' for Barbie's on my door,
in shiny pink. It's
stuck with Blue Tack
which oozes out.

It's not like what's inside:
books, paper, writing desk,
certificates, pictures,
collected things.

I keep thinking I'll take it off.
It doesn't suit my room,
my bit of space,
my bit of me.

But this careful, careless 'B'
just keeps whispering about,
not what's inside, but what's outside
and therefore inside too.

For all she cares
who stuck it up, my room
could be an empty space,
except when I'm in there.

Glass of Blessings

After George Herbert, 'The Pulley'

God made man
in all respects and therefore
all his gifts, his faults, his powers,
are of God, if not, wherefrom?
Therefore if he fall, or fail
how might he do other?
Did God then toss His creature
into the world and blame him
for what He made?

Paper Train

You'd never guess who I was sitting next to
the other day on the train! It was that poet,
Armstead is it? Stephen? Anyway
after a while I noticed he was
leaning across a little bit
and trying to see what I was reading.
I ignored him and turned away;
I didn't want him to see what I was looking at -
whas'name's, you know the one's,
review of recent poetry: according to her,
most of it 'lacks meaningful content'
and Armstrong's work 'was no exception'.

As we began to slow down
I closed the book emphatically
and looked out of the window.
We soon drew into ... that's funny I thought,
the station name boards were blank!
'Aah', said the poet, 'we're here'.

Afterlife

Edward the Confessor d.1066, Flying Scotsman,
refurbished 2016

He prayed that his spirit might fly unimpeded
to the realm of heavenly souls, that
golden place tinkling with unearthly music
where there is only love and peace.

The celestial vapours of that resurrected
behemoth shriek from out of sight, then,
in a thunderbolt of instant presence,
vouchsafe a glimpse of what is not of this world.

Oh, Edward, on his knees in the royal chapel.
Oh, passengers, adoring their gins and tonics.
Oh, heirless England.
Oh, doting trackside watchers,
opaque, shambling goods train.

Head of Leon Kossoff

Frank Auerbach, 1954

Moon hands down judgment
in despair. Heaped
with ashes, earth rains
rivers of tears. Paint thrown,
plastered, dripping, cannot obscure.

Plum pudding with chocolate sauce
sweats in steam.

A Man Embracing a Woman

Dosso Dossi, c.1524

I'm past Gibraltar and into home seas.
Failing freak storms—by no means impossible—
I'll be docking at St Marks tomorrow morning,
my fortune made. I'm wearing black—
I would not tempt providence
which might yet smite me. The weather's
set fair for now, the storm damage repaired,
new sails hoist.   And all because of this
lovely creature. I've adorned her with flowers
and these charming clothes. She's mine!

Who has decked me with Morning Glory?
Who or what do they think I am—
some nymph of a tree or grotto?
My place is there, with the seals and dolphins
and the uncountable fish. Nereus
sent me to this ship in trouble. I defeated the
storm nymphs and despatched them to their island
where they lie in sorrow and exhaustion.
And now I find myself here. I ache
with longing for my home in the silvery cave.
Who is this oaf with his arm round me?

João Gilberto in Rio

Compli-
cated
city.
A strang-
er takes
your hand
and leads
you through
streets and
alleys,
through av-
enues
and parks—
'this way
my friend,
along
this path,
turn here
and up
this track'—
and leads
you back
to where
you start-
ed from.

*Note: Joao Gilberto is the Brazilian singer and guitarist who established the
new genre of Bossa Nova in the late 1950s.*

23

Billy Strayhorn's Journey

1. Take the A Train

Hull up it cuts the surface water beating the prow slaps rhythmically as dark blue hull sears through waves slapping in rhythm screw beats rhythm drives the boat through green through translucent blue through flecks of sun orange flickers of deep brown the spray translucently dancing against solid glistening dark blue shears through surfaces, black shape below.

2. Upper Manhattan Medical Group

Currents twist and loop past strange boulders leaning in sand of curious intensity, mixed and separate, stark and faint, while sea plants of hallucinatory silhouette slip and tangle, seaweed, dark and secret, streams.

Pickpocket poet

In the café of the gallery, Americano,
pear and chocolate cake, BEWARE
OF PICKPOCKETS.

Upper Norwood in winter.
Figures in the snow ... Smash!

of cunning plate
Eh? What?
My poem! Racing out
past dancers, living statues,
past contortionists,
me in hot pursuit
he, scribbling on the run.

I need them words,
'Norwood', what's that when it's at home?
Stop thief! Pick up that word.
Grab him, he's got my poem!
But he's slippery, and writing, writing.
Winter now he doesn't like
and tosses it away
and still he runs and still I chase,
and still the crowd just gapes.
Rugby tackle, grab it back:

Smithfield, dawn, it's
freeze your bum time.
Bloody rain

I let him go.

'A Tremendous Jape'

Historian MRD Foot describing an operation
led by Major Patrick Leigh Fermor in Crete, 1944

Everyone was your friend, made you
their children's godfather, made you
uniforms, so you could flag down the car,
knock out the driver and bundle
the general into the back.
You donned his cap, wore it
with such insouciance, employed
your language skills with such effect,
that you sailed through the checkpoints,
twenty of them! What a whizz! Not

that everything went exactly to plan:
the Butcher of Crete,
General Friedrich Wilhelm Müller,
was elsewhere, and what you got
was 'Harmless Heinrich' Kreipe
sullenly muttering Horace:
Vides ut alta ... Look there,
deep under sparkling snow, Soracte stands;

and the Butcher came racing back
with the tools of his trade

but you were equal to the challenge:
　　　... nec iam sustineant ... her groaning trees
you said to Heinrich
　　　　　can hardly bear the load
and all her streams are blocked with ice.

Petticoat

For Marie Jalowicz Simon, b. 1922, d. 1998

The visitors,
Immaculate in grey,
march into her bedroom.
'Oh, may I first just make a sandwich for the journey?
Come, I will hardly run off in my petticoat!'

Which is what she does and is
taken in, sheltered
passed on, taken in again,
fed and clothed,
hidden, taken in,
sheltered.

Time passes, a regime falls
and in the confusion,
in the hunger,
in the shame, she is designated
Official Survivor. And such
have a right to be housed.

'Come, you can hardly expect me
to live in a house with a shell hole
for a roof!' So she must walk
and walk and walk
past skeletons of houses,
along remains of roads,
through devastated woods,
to a house with a roof that the stars shine on,
rather than through. 'Hello dear
water-tap'. She washes her feet.
She stretches out.
She sleeps.

Let's go!

Church, sandwich, and
on your bikes for a ride to Southend
on the weedy concrete of the roadside
cycle track, Dennis lorries staggering
past, black-wreathed in the sun,
biscuits and tea when you get there,
come back, come back slow, tanned, relaxed
for supper, bed and tomorrow. Tomorrow
you must turn your heart black as sin,
as the Ace of Spades, as fresh cut coal,
sign up, sign up for the King, to
sail the seas, learn to drill, thrill
to the roaring sky, kill
or be killed.

Back the Attack—Buy Bonds

from a photograph (New York, USA, 1943)

Back the attack.
Back the attack.
Smash that butterhead.
Snap his scrawny neck.

Behind the counter, under the banner, pose
for flashgunned Speed Graphics, Contaxes, girls:
smart girls, girls in uniform, bond-selling girls,
all-American, all black.

Back the attack
until the Jap cracks.
Then lady get back,
get back, get back.

Divine Wind

Monsters, gorillas,
ugly, clumsy, godless,
want everything,
want to starve, destroy, sacred Japan.
Throw your savage fire at me, me,
my plane and I are sturdy, nimble,
we weave and duck, shake off blows,
nearer, nearer.

Emperor, duty, father's pride.
Emperor looked on, smiled a little maybe,
I am part, I am part.
How we worked, passed out with pride,
our uniforms beautiful,
same and beautiful, lines of white gloves.
Now the red sun adorns my forehead.
We ran, ran, fell, scrambled up,
laughed and laughed.
Instructor hard like rock, never stopped, shouting, shouting,
but proud of us his sons and proud
that we stand for the fatherland.
Into our planes, solo for the first time,
we sing into the air—all Japan can see.

Bucks and rocks as air explodes,
steady, steady,
not my hands that shake.

Matsuko, my sweet bride,
looks down then shyly up.
Kneeling, she spoons rice into bowls,
for me, for child, children.

nearer, nearer.
I see men.

One Fine Day

for Cio-Cio-san

Sharpless, the consul, long retired, is now in a home in a pleasant part of Oahu not far from Honolulu city. Although a little out of his wits these days he can hear above him a sound like a multitude of angry insects and wonders what it might be.

Lieutenant Commander George Washington Pinkerton (birth name Sorrow) is on the bridge of the *Arizona* at Pearl with Captain Van Valkenburgh and other senior officers. They too can hear a distant hum.

Interior with a Lady Choosing Fish

Quiringh van Brekelenkam, 1664

The seated woman. The servant girl
offering the white flesh. The solid chairs,
the clock, the picture in its gilt frame.
The man in the doorway who may not enter.

The best he can do is hover above the surface,
waiting for a bite, his hook and line
perfectly placed. His intended victim
examines the bait but hasn't taken. In any case
she's too much for him.

Even the servant girl looks too well turned out
but he may be able to reel her in. He smells
of fish, he looks like a beggar, he's old.
But she has nothing. Even her clothes
are her employer's.   Better bite now
while she has a chance.

Brighton Pierrots

Walter Sickert, 1915

Arms akimbo, hat pushed back,
he peers out at no-men-left-land
fearing they've cratered.
But the show must go on —
he's softened them up
with a barrage of jokes
and is ready to go.

A white bird, its feathers
stretched like a plane's wings
Is looking for something. France
glows red in the distance.
The pierrots wait in reserve.

Cafferty's lunch

The truck gravels to a stop.
Crows bounce and scramble,
hop and argue, their black shapes
black against glabrous grass,
toothless fence, fuliginous tree.
The truck sneezes awake,
continues on its way. The crows
discuss a crumpled paper bag.

Trains

What have we done to deserve trains:
their hereness and goneness,
their doors open to let people off and on
and closedness, their swish of greeting,
roar of farewell, their sheer presence, at least
the grand, important ones that go
to places like Truro and Lostwithiel?

When a train stands throbbing with easy purpose
in an Edward Thomas country station
like Castle Cary set in an unpeopled valley
demonstrating the law of perspectives,
twice if you stand in the middle,
there's a frisson, a connectedness.
Then clouds of blue-grey diesel
where it isn't any more
and birds settling back into trees.

Terra Nullius

after David Harsent, 'M.A.D.'

Or it might be dinosaurs which emerge again
after the long quietus, as the world
slips back to normal.

Eons after its unwanted guests have left
there will be room for all kinds
as long as one is absent.

     *

And space will slowly clear, allowing
the moon and stars to shine again
through a clear sky, though no-one will notice

except God,
who might howl for his loss,
though no-one will hear.

     *

It was one point five. It was trumped.
No turning back. Ice wailed.
Waters rose. It rained for forty days

or never rained again, at least not
while earth's denizens skittered and slid
off the world's slippery end.

Fawley Bottom

i.m. the Pipers

Down there, at the end of the track
by the swamp-like cimmerian Thames,
Myfanwy eking the last of the light
into *Death in Venice* as the kettle bristles
and the beef stew murmurs
its mysterious music, you are applying
those singing blues and yellows
near the things they belong to,
the translucent colours leading the eye
to objects which are not quite there.

The Listening Girl

Jean-Baptiste Greuze, 1780s

I'm pretty as a picture: my clothes
and lips precisely match
my artfully messy hair. One breast's
half exposed. I'm seventeen. I'm
every man's coy fantasy, meaning
I'm too innocent to imagine
what you have in mind.

Girls should be seen only and listen,
my pose confirms it—it's not just
that you have the right ... , but that
I'm eager to hear what you have to say.

But if you'd stop gaping at me like that,
paused your nonsense for five minutes
and listened yourself for a change, well,
who knows what you might hear?

Over There

I went over there to visit my father
and, as we had before in another place,
we walked the streets, he showing me
things he had discovered after his move there.
Somewhat to my surprise there were paintings
in all the streets: 'Look at this, Rob,
that pale blue, that sweep of blanched orange,
how lovely they are together; that girl, the way
she's looking at ..., the stillness of those pears'.
And then we stood for a while in front of a
harbour scene: cargo boats shifting
gently in the swell were unloading at the quays
while tugs and smaller craft scuttled busily about.
Groups of men, chattering, grunting, moved
to and from the moored vessels carrying bales
and sides of beef and pork, pushing trolleys,
driving trucks. All was bustle, noise and smoke
amidst the constant sound of waves lapping
at the piers. A solitary man in an overcoat
stood with his back to us, looking out over
the water. We looked and looked, the man,
the watching man, not ever turning round.

Bus

It sailed past me,
the bus from Portadown
to Princeton Street, leaving me
well-nigh apoplectic.

I'm thinking that buses never come
on time unless you're
running late, and then, like as not,
after they've plunged
through the puddle you're racing past,
they pause just long enough
to give you time to establish that, yes,
that was the one you wanted.

The Girl

She paused for a moment on the stairs,
then went in through the station entrance
and I was left with a memory
of her ordinary beauty. That image
would last a lifetime or at least
until the next willow-like
and flowing girl entered my sight.

I would have had her meet someone
out of sight, bringing him
a swift and loving smile to light up his face
as he reached to carry her bag.
Then they would stroll together
onto the platform and wait
to be transported to another place, one
beneath the trees by a river or sea-shore.

She paused for a moment, and I
imagined her turning her head,
not to see icily through me but to give me
a smile she really meant, inscribing
a moment on my mind, one
filled with beauty, and possibly even
containing a suggestion of truth.

Borders

after David Jones, 'The Dying Gaul'

You listen to *Today*, you read *the Guardian*
and think you understand, but you don't,
how could you? You would not be able
to think—however hard you tried -
the way *it* does, the Clarendon Priesthood.

       From house to work
       from work to house ...
But you realise something as you
       crawl down St Peters Hill,
       suffer the bridge, inch
       past the fortifications of
       the inner distribution road.
For years and years
       on the Great West Road
       negotiating innumerable staging posts.
You're forced to wonder sometimes about
those outside the *limes,*
       back and forth,
       for twenty or thirty years
to the outer reaches of its sway.

Sometimes you think you'll join them,
jump ship, so to speak, find out
what they think of its inscrutable machinations
and of us its skivvies,
discover what they might be cogitating out there.

Immaculate Conception

Velasquez, 1619

Gold and white clouds
in a cobalt sky;
a sweet, solemn face
with downcast eyes;
soft abundant hair; folds
in a glowing silk gown.
The conception immaculate.
The delivery flawless.

Conclusions

I don't think there were any plans for me. Only,
my mum and dad wanted my happiness,
probably to be found, they thought,
in job, marriage, and children. Education
was the key and we went for it
hammer and tongs. What we didn't realise
was that education makes promises
that life isn't obliged to keep, that when you exit
your turnstile, pockets stuffed
with praise, attention and good will,

you will suddenly find yourself in a place
that is wholly strange to you. You look
in your pocket for a map but there isn't one.
There are no signposts, there's nobody
to guide you or tell you where to go
and one direction seems as good as another.
You hang around, wondering what to do
and eventually some kind of bus appears.
You may as well get on. It lurches off.
Hang on tight! Hang on for dear life!

Intimations

Sliced bread, canned rice pudding,
two bottles of beer, all manner of
worn out viscera,
memories and forgettings
weigh him down.

Skateboarded youths
whizz round his head like wasps,
poke him with attitude.
Their species is different.
They are immortal.

The Bore

Next day I bumped into Half-Past Four. He was a bore.
                    Carol Ann Duffy, 'Meeting Midnight'

I *am*
a bore at half past four but I've
hours to go in this sodding
place and
I don't get home
till nearly eight, then I'm
whacked. So
it's takeaway time
with a glass of wine
or two
or more
and I start to feel right
and ready for the night
and it's down the pub
to meet the boys,
wade into the noise
feel more and more
much less of a bore.

Excitement in the Garden

Nothing untoward here:
Trees explode slowly
Grass perdures
Birdsong: 62 decibels
Fence stops too much escaping
Sky stops too much growing
Pause at pre-spring

Fox!
gone
Dachshund! (dachshund!?)
gone

Calm down garden!

Abbey Quarter

A woman with a baby
makes the complicated
transition
from seated to upright.
A young man
helps her with her bag,
passing the strap over
her head, carefully
avoiding fingers, child,
nose and glasses. This
in *The Cloisters*
coffee bar near where
the abbot was hanged, then
drawn and quartered.

Body And Soul

All I know is I just had a way of playing and
I didn't think in terms of any other instrument
but the tenor

Coleman Hawkins

Iron framed bed, double-breasted suit,
overcoat, pork pie hat, winter shoes,
New York Times, wash-stand,
basin, shaving gear, glass of water,
brown bag with apples, Jack Daniels,
saxophone case, gramophone, LPs:
Bach cello suites—Tortellier
Bach cello suites—Casals

How to Write a Poem

For UH

First, fill your space with cherry blossom,
grass of glowing green, colourful flowers
of all kinds. Let there be
a sparkling stream, returning birds
skating on the bright air.

Place a black tree to the side,
its trunk cropped by the margin.

Let Mount Fuji
peep between its branches.

Portrait

after 115 sittings Cezanne said that 'he was not
discontented with the front of the shirt'

He's like a dog at a fence,
prowling, snarling, patrolling. He turns
back, turns back, turns back, searching
for an opening which is not there.
The more it's not there, the more he looks.

Vollard sits, he sits again. He sits
a hundred times and more
while he unfinishes it. Meanwhile
he growls at landscapes, searching
for a way into them, a way there is not.

Vallier sits, as he prowls toward death.
Who knows how many times?
Who knows what discontents?
All we can know is that Vallier
and landscape have merged
into the same opacity.

There is a clifftop

after Thomas Campion, 'There is a Garden in Her Face'

There is a clifftop in her face
of glowing green, of charming rocks
of limpid pools and breeze-stirred fields of gold,
of tender paths which stroll their ways
in easeful pleasure, far above
the envious main

which rubbernecks and flings
its irritated self, flings and flings again
in helpless furious spite at the cliff's foot.
That head meanwhile, that beauteous face
preening itself amongst th'adoring clouds,
looks down in majesty upon the lowly sea

which stretches out in horizontal impotence
that would be vertical. Time, the while,
whose only pleasure is to plot,
eyes the towering cliff with a grim smile,
regardless of the spiteful sea,
its sometime ally, not needed here and now.

Il Postino

i.m. Massimo Troisi

Your Mario found life, love, new life
and death. And as if to emphasise the last,
yours swiftly followed.

The sound of the waves,
the wind in the trees,
the great bell tolling ...

And Pablito, named for the poet,
would be grown now,
were he not immortal.

The Heart's Reason

Morton Schamberg: Untitled (Mechanical Abstraction), 1916

This heart has only reason.
The artist's heart,
which is not in it,
has reasons of its own
of which this heart
knows nothing.

Dogs, Dead Game and Fruit

Alexandre-Francois Desportes, 1715

the world is full of absent men
and the birds they shot
and the fruit they plucked
and the ruins they built
and dogs